BY DINAH LIVINGSTONE

POETRY

Pamphlets:
Beginning (1967)
Tohu Bohu (1968)
Maranatha (1969)
Ultrasound (1974)
Prepositions and Conjunctions (1977)
Love in Time (1982)
Glad Rags (1983)
Something Understood (1985)
St Pancras Wells (1991)

Books:
Saving Grace (1987)
Keeping Heart - Poems 1967-89 (1989)
Second Sight (1993)

Edited:
Camden Voices Anthology 1978-1990 (1990)

PROSE

Poetry Handbook for Readers and Writers (1992)

MAY DAY

MAY DAY

Dinah Livingstone

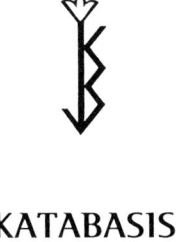

KATABASIS

First published in 1997 by KATABASIS
10 St Martins Close, London NW1 0HR (0171 485 3830)
Copyright: Dinah Livingstone 1997
Cover and illustrations by Anna Mieke Lumsden
Printed and bound by SRP, Exeter (01296 29271)
Proof read by Grace Livingstone

Trade Distribution: Password Books
23 New Mount Street
Manchester M4 4DE (0161 953 4009)

ISBN: 0 904872 27 0

British Library Cataloguing in Publication Data:
A catalogue record for this book is available
from the British Library.

KATABASIS is grateful for the support
of the London Arts Board.

Certainly May Day is above all days of the year fitting for the protest of the disinherited against the system of robbery that shuts the door betwixt them and a decent life; the day when the promise of the year reproaches the waste inseparable from the society of inequality . . .

Look how the whole capital world is stretching out long arms . . . and grabbing and clutching in eager competition . . . for the opening of fresh markets to take in all the fresh profit-producing wealth which is growing greater and greater every day; in other words, to make fresh opportunities for *waste*; the waste of our labour and our lives.

And I say this is an irresistible instinct on the part of capitalists, an impulse like hunger, and I believe that it can only be met by another hunger, the hunger for freedom and fair play for all, both people and peoples.

William Morris
Article in *Justice*, May 1st 1896

ACKNOWLEDGMENTS

Some of these poems have appeared in the following newspapers, magazines and anthologies:

Acumen, Agenda, Camden New Journal, Completing the Picture, Daily Express, Ramraid Extraordinaire, Rive Gauche Anthology, Sea of Faith Magazine, Tears in the Fence, The Poet's Voice.

CONTENTS

May Day	1
Work	2
Flexible	4
Emergency	6
Hurtling Where?	8
Trees be Company	9
Bagley Combe	11
Aldgate	14
Blank	15
Marks of Woe	16
Intimations of Utopia	17
Grey Day	18
The Prize	20
At Home	22
Virtue	24
Lonely Began	26
Fellow Creatures	28
Defeat	31
The Purple-Headed Mountain	33
Going to Work	36
English Lesson	38
Like	39
The Divine Image	40
Private Hell	41
Body of Work	42
Gothic	45
Because	47
The Excluded	50
To My Old Friend Hugo Meynell	52
Risk	58
Pressure of Life	59
In Avery Hill Park	60
This	61
Maytime	62
NOTES	64

MAY DAY

A May morning at Minsmere,
in the bird reserve, many calls
I can't identify — some singing,
some sound more conversational
and the bass is the rhythm of the sea.

Before me in young leaf the May tree
stands frothing with starry blossom,
milky sunlit epiphany:
in admiration hope does not fail.

The tree is thick and squat,
its comfortable shape,
tousled on top,
spikes the hazy blue
now clearing to speedwell.

Its flowering month
opens with that annual outburst
of belief in life before death,
faith leading to insight
of a species as whole-heartedly human
as it is most tranquilly tree.

Of course they want to cancel it.
These bosses despise
workers, makers, seers,
deny their holiday.
Time runs out on earth.
May Day. May Day. May Day . . .

WORK

In my street I saw eight pigeons
feasting on the fruits of a whitebeam tree.
They nestled among the yellowing leaves
like outsize dusky plums.
I saw a squirrel run along a fence,
then down it to dig in leafmould,
busy to bury its winter hoard.

On a windy walk I saw willows
waving by the river near the weir.
Tart, luscious blackberries
clustered on wet brambles in the hedge
and a dying-back briar bore rosehips
aching vermilion like stained glass,
whose ripeness blazed to burst
with seed for birds, syrup for babies,
but first to renew its kind.

The earth does its work,
produces bread, that smells good,
and beauty; life for its own sake
and human tongues to speak for it.
Poems are called works because of this:
the ground which grew us has decreed
in every faculty, efforts, however fierce,
to feed and keep ourselves, crave and create
delight, that is distinct not separate.
Grace no less than bread defines
desire's economy, abounding
like lambs in spring, squirrels in London,
and kindly satisfied.

In another street I saw young beggars,
who had neither bread nor bed,
which I didn't give.
I put my plastic in the cash machine:
Your request has not been authorised,
it said. How to get by
with no money? I rang the bank
five times. Each time a different clerk,
trained in frantic figures to maintain the fence
between have-nots and haves,
produced nothing but frustration,
or the computers were down.
Not working. Unkind.

FLEXIBLE

Jaded, fagged, fit for the knackers,
my body sags, my stomach aches,
acid from weeks of tense work-seeking,
offers that keep collapsing, chasing
odd teaching hours in colleges
dotted about the city, take it or leave it,
reach it by dodgy tube, creaking,
trundling journey, interrupted constantly.
Though the term has barely started,
distressed, unpaid, exhausted,
I badly need a holiday.

Today on the first Sunday of October
after a brisk walk to clear my head,
I rest in this ancient garden
washed and shaken by equinoctial gales,
where the revitalised grass flares
brilliant emerald. I am calmed
by the tearful hedged formality,
sobbing now subsided,
as breezy azure sunshine warms us dry.

A squirrel creeps along the bench,
sits up and begs. I have nothing for it,
no titbits, feel more akin to that
battered patch of Michaelmas daisies.

They say they want their workforce flexible.
Indeed my bones feel limp;
a lonely sack of swept-up leaves,
all friends deferred, I am just too tired.
I pray the nerve massacre is over.
Golden air now mellow me.
Swishing numinous trees be my archangels.

EMERGENCY

University College Hospital
is sentenced to death by a kangaroo court.
My last child was born there.
Later, stretching to paint a ceiling,
I fell off a careless coupling of milk crates
and smashed my elbow joint to smithereens.
They mended it. It could have remained
robotically rigid forever.

We indignant locals rallied
with the nurses on strike against extinction,
cheered the speakers — the North West London
postmen delivered first class support.
We marched to the Middlesex —
more speeches and shouting
and patients clapping at windows.
Then the cry: 'All march back to UCH!'

In their neat blue print dresses
and sensible shoes, the nurses led,
spreading across the whole width
of rush-hour Tottenham Court Road.
Police were pleading till one,
in an impatient overtaking,
hopped his panda along the pavement
to get in front and contain the spirit.

Nurses trained to respond
to emergency, with one mind, without
a second's hesitation nipped ahead,
mostly young women,
in admirable co-operation,
maintaining control of the street.
Now they were chanting:
'The workers united will never be defeated!'

1993

HURTLING WHERE?

The danger appals
as bungling managers,
mostly accountants,
give the wrong signals.

We do not need more cars
consuming land for roads,
poisoning us with fumes.
Give us health and safety,
competence and common sense,
not greed to run the country.

Give us the professionals.
Support the signal workers.
Give them their due.
They keep us on the rails.

1994

TREES BE COMPANY

1

All these miserable dog days
spent prisoner, bossed in an arid office
by a more than usually distasteful capitalist —
ruthless egotist and religious with it —
she has been greenhoused,
azure-blued by a haze of longing,
glazed airless away from cool
waters to lap her body,
grass to stretch out on.
Frazzled and addled, her brain too
is a trek through a desert of clinker.

A high cost to pay for her crust to his profit.
For if he has sold his soul to Mammon,
here in one of its sweltering dens,
it has also obtained, as part of the deal,
a lease on his underlings. Surplus value.

2

I have been saved by the trees.
Through my left window the ash
dangles its bunches of keys
growing ripe for unlocking.
There stands the self-possessed poplar,
with its trunk's wrinkled geography
uprushing but chunky − unlike its lanky
Lombardy cousin − and its skyscape
a wide oval, consoling globe
full of leaves, many hearts never still,
who subversively whisper to keep me alive.

This afternoon after weeks of heatwave
at last the weather is gusty,
my trees are swishing deliciously,
maybe a storm blowing up,
while I am here wishing.

BAGLEY COMBE

I have come back to Bagley Combe.
This year mid-August the rowan is still ripening
and its neighbour may tree,
a greater presence than I remember,
has haws still raw.

Refreshing me from the sound of traffic,
the clear brown water rushes down
between banks where the long grass tangles
with deep gold birdsfoot trefoil,
splashes of purple heather, whortleberry
leaves beginning to blush,
reeds, thistles, cow parsley, interesting ferns.

I sit on soft sloping turf,
still dewy in places, with drops on little webs,
and dotted with rock roses' delicate yellow stars.
I try to avoid the rabbit droppings,
though they are dry and flaking back to earth.
Earth who basks in the morning sun
warming her bracken body hair,
that seems to exude her smell.

I lie still, belonging here
as just another life form she has grown.
I become part of the scenery.
Two rapid walkers –
speaking a North American dialect,
I wonder idly what tribe they are –
tramp down to the little ford,
over and up the other side
and do not notice me. I am glad.

Now I hear the grasshopper get busy
and all sorts of bird calls
I wish I understood.
This peaceful earth is energetic
with all her secret growth.
And peaceful here as part of her,
I rest at the heart of my life,
my purest energy, my most loving will.

All verbiage would break the silence,
the burdensome poundage of the Sunday papers,
even the prose I thought of producing
earlier this year, now seem too noisy.
But wording is part of my nature
and just as the grasshopper's chitter
and the stream rushing
increase the sense of repose,
my only recourse is poetry.
I invite it to visit me now
to stress and intensify.

The placard I carried recently —
Poets Support the Right to Silence —
was for justice,
against the Criminal Justice Bill.
And they danced in the fountains for liberty.
I have contributed so little
but out of the great silence
of the earth's eternal delight,
with all my will I want the promise kept:

For humanity not to fall short
of its poetry, the comfort
and pleasure it can imagine for everyone —
not just the gross and greedy few —
for the misery and waste to be over,
our whole species free to enjoy
the economy of its quiet earth,
obviously, naturally, as trees by water
whose clustering berries and haws turn red
when it's time, for the poem
the whole heart's reason resting here
cannot help raising — requiring an answer —
to become active, archway,
shimmering vista, word in deed.

So fellow creatures, when this large woman
outcrop of Exmoor landscape
comes home to London,
ruddy and weathered,
let me be building material.

ALDGATE

It is as if the gate still stood.
At this point police put up their cordon.
Where from Stepney, the Commercial Road
with its little claustrophobic family grocers,
its cheap wholesale clothing shops
displaying their blouses, bright dresses and saris,
merges with the millenial route
past Mile End council flats, Whitechapel street stalls,
and together they hit the City —
Fenchurch Street, Lloyds, Leadenhall Market —
immediately the buildings change,
become bigger, richer, solider, quieter.
At that junction, or rather confrontation,
stands St Botolph-without-Aldgate
(he was a Suffolk man and travellers' patron).

In the crypt there is a homeless project
with a day centre and canteen.
Unlike the tidy, scurrying office workers,
often its patrons lounging in the yard
look scruffy and derelict, sometimes shout.
Behind the altar of the ancient church,
rebuilt in mundane eighteenth century style,
blazes a focal modern batik
portraying the precious-stone foundations
of well-met, four-gated new Jerusalem,
its river watering the tree of life that bears
twelve red fruits of ripened hope.
Built both heart in heart and hand in hand,
the transfigured golden city in the background
has a silhouette that could be London.

BLANK

I wake up to snow,
furry flakes falling on my window sill,
trees and ledges. Seagulls wheeling
and calling Camden Town.
A little black thicket in the branches opposite
is a bare nest. The street is sheeted.
Last night's lurid urgent dream
grows dim. So much I wanted to say
now blanketed. I contemplate
the rest of this white page.

MARKS OF WOE

Dark February doubtful daylight,
through dreary rain and sludge
I trudge to Camden tube,
clumsily jump black pools
where the drains are defective,
stumble over cracked lumpy paving,
afraid I'll fall in filth, get hurt.

The ticket hall is hub
to those already supping Super Tennants
and homeless hoping for the price
of a breakfast cuppa,
who implore me. Pressured
I ignore them feeling cruel.

The down escalator is not working.
Giddily I descend the grim spiral,
slippery to the trains. A lugubrious voice:
'Kings Cross Station is closed.' Again.
The via-Bank service lurches,
crunches to a halt in the tunnel.

We customers are used to it,
sit hunched in the dark
blocked drain,
dreary and private
with closed February faces.

INTIMATIONS OF UTOPIA

Bleak March night in Camden Town.
Few people are awake yet
to face the forthcoming infuriation
of the misery line.

But very early
while it is still dark
the birds start singing
what it is to be alive.

Snug under duvet drowsily
I distinguish a blackbird
thrilling between riff,
recitative and liquid air.

The crowded city chorus
does not drown a single voice.
Such happiness on earth.
Can this be London? Nowhere else.

Hark the herald
feathering the thought nest
of that future blissful daybreak,
which will hatch struggling.

Warmbreasted
fellow earthling
mothers hope, music
I must believe.

GREY DAY

On a grey morning
everything is so ordinary.
My beloved plane trees fret,
sunless and dull without spirit.

There is no good news in the paper.
The government continues
to get away with it,
marketing itself with its wonted waffle,
selling something else off, short-changing
us ordinary people again.

Our voice grows fainter and duller,
while their gang gets fatter
and stronger as usual
snuffling hog-plums in quangos.

At breakfast
my bank manager's letter
becomes more threatening
(and he charges £27.50 for it).
I remain in the red.

Sunless and dull without spirit,
I realise the change
won't happen today.
The odds are hopeless.

Nevertheless I remain
red, where the heart is and danger
and, streaking out of the grey
shifted clouds, sunset on this
so-called new world order
and that sunrise I so hunger for.

THE PRIZE

April in Kew Gardens.
Against the hazy azure of desire,
presses newness of gauzy green.
The tree my bench is under
has little catkins, tender leaves unpleating.
Delightful far-flung archipelago,
daffodil islands gild my gaze.
Through them the iridescent pheasant strides,
cock in his splendid vain testosterone,
pursued by a stumbling stocky lad,
a yearning four-year-old,
about to be disappointed.

This morning I saw Cerón win the marathon
and as I ambled down the Mall,
up Birdcage Walk, the tens of thousands
straining after him.
Gasping along the Embankment
with only a mile to go,
the innocent, vivid-vested, sweaty medley
grasped their last drink
across from sold-off County Hall.

Though I am idling on this garden seat,
my recollection is not tranquil.
I am as English as the daffodils
or cockney runners in eccentric kit,
but the hazy childhood story
I was floated in − this island
as a kind safe place, the misty trust
injustices were easily put right
by common sense and decency −

disperses in the hard glare of London now,
privatised, corrupt, collapsing capital.
Sleazy England races to defeat its competitors,
with shifty and feckless goal a wasted earth.
Uneasy eyes avoid a human face.

The raucous pheasant calls:
Look up! Look up!
There shines the golden city of kindness,
longing intense as April
sap rising in us.
Then the hurt heart fills with pleasure,
pressing till common sense
dances with the daffodils.

AT HOME

The oak is gnarled and old,
its solid trunk has deeply furrowed bark.
Marvellous again in May
its pointed nut-brown buds
swell and sprout their lemon-lacy,
tenderly unfolding little leaves
and happily dangling catkins
from knobby branches skewing
every which way against the breezy sky.
Standing alone in a meadow, self-possessed,
it takes its full majestic shape.
Rooks flap over its ample crown.

Earth now greening with young root crops,
upward the mild ploughland gently curves
in a soft sensual parabola.
I walk over its wide brow,
where from the top I see two villages
and hear skylarks cascading through clear air.
Then down a narrow lane
I come upon a bank of cow parsley
with a grey uprushing ash,
whose flowers flare like starbursts
and leaf bunches thrust out crown imperials
from tiny tight black cloven hooves.

More oaks opposite edge an enchanted copse.
Entering, I suddenly endure a paradisal
azure of infinite imaginings,
faintly perfumed, shock of bluebells
plunging sharply to a marshy stream.
Pheasants squawk. Frogs croak.

Squirrels chase each other along high branches,
enjoying their springing agility
and more birds sing.

England I love so dearly,
your oaks and sister ash
are choked by greedy ivy;
I fear your magic wood is dying,
sold to the idolised obscene demon
demanding daily human sacrifice,
while your mellow cattle that for centuries
have given good roast beef
are poisoned.

Prophets are banished
and your huge language, gnarled and old,
instead of being renewed,
is logged for fuel
to fix the fast food
falsity of titbit and soundbite,
create acres of pretty repeat
wallpaper poetry
concealing the rot within.

VIRTUE

I heard you read last night
your shining finished poem.
I heard you, your spirit
ringing true, clear bell
more beautiful than angel
because embodied and belonging
to this earth. Words
from your mouth and brain and breath.

Echo of the future possible
each voice most itself,
speaking its most self
and being felt by listeners
answering in kind.
These are the poems of the city,
nowhere yet,
but now here at odd conjunctions.

I've heard it sometimes
at the Working Men's College
and such humble London gatherings,
glimpsed a human garden
growing happily together
with earth's other creatures,
beloved trees and graceful animals.
Like May Day my cat.

What social joys are there,
music, supper, song of songs,
after the long haul,
after the deep shared pleasure
when we see off the dominant hobgoblins,
witness their grotesque Idol
implode like Mr Blobby
in the twinkling of an eye.

What I've heard I see.
Is any true poetry without
the sheen of utopia,
green sunlight on morning dew,
encouraging seed now buried
in the ground for hope?

Why is the bloom of beauty
so deeply desired?
Why is earth sighing till softly
dew falls on the opening flower?
Mother earth groaning for that new morning
to break with its lamb-like cry?

LONELY BEGAN

Now in winter she is
a drizzling island with no visitors.
What is the point of outpouring
unwanted poems,
which are becoming non-language
because no one listens?

She chatters at her cat
and whistles to blackbirds
but you don't need words
for that. Words want hearers.

Futile to turn to God
in her isolation.
He cannot comfort her
he is fiction, an old doll.

Even a cat, breathing warm fur,
is kinder company than that
mouthing in her mirror
at her own hard glass reflection.

Worse than the ignominy
of being ignored,
blanked as if she had never been,
is the silence self-imposed,
choosing to be mute,
       unvoiced,
              petering out,
having lost conviction
that what she says can matter.

Isn't it just
a thin patter faltering to a halt,
a dying fall fading?

Loneliness lessens her.
She dwindles.
The deep void yawns.
What stops her short is sheer —
however faintly felt today
and muffled by thick grief —
faith in the tongue she shares,
surely with fellow speakers somewhere.

Sea gusts taste salty,
her eyes sting.
Forlorn in the teatime dusk,
her footstep crunches shingle
along the dismal shore.
She shouts to hear herself,
then ships her embottled words
across the bitter waters.

FELLOW CREATURES

'Fellow creature' was a common mode of address used by the Diggers

1

Dapple on velvet,
the young black cat with golden ripples
appropriates the ornate, high-backed
intricately carved oak chair,
stretches herself on its faded plush
mulberry-fool upholstery,
claims her legitimate throne
her sleeping seat.

In stillness after midnight
solitude's deep root flowers.
Outburst alleluia from the earth:
'Glory *here*, Diggers all!'
The burring chorus blazes
as humble humanity,
now marigold-haloed,
finally makes it home.

In darkness the moment of seeing,
hearing the not yet uttered.
Kneel on the silky mat
where two white harts stand
under a noble tree. I rest my head
against the chairback's padding.
A surprise bunch fills my arms:
the cat purrs, pulse of the universe.

2

These days every afternoon
heatwaves ripple over Hampstead Heath.
Laid back in the Ladies' Pond I gaze up
at blue through willow. I turn over
and with slow breast stroke continue.
A duck swims towards me speedy and neat.
I admire her elegant economy
and engage her kingcup-yellow eye.
Velvet water laps her as it laps me,
animals in one of our elements.
Two feet from my face
she veers off to the left.

Some swimmers have come here regularly
for years. Some leathery now
have seen much of the century,
might have been suffragettes
still battling on, benevolent pond spirits.
Solid as willow trunk in middle age,
sometimes I'm accompanied by nymphs,
my daughters – rosebay and water lily –
mermaid hair floats like weed.
Generations of useful bodies
in all their various modes.
Comfort of women.

On the walk back, a glimpse of men
doing flash acrobatics
from their pond's diving board.
Shock of difference. Sudden tension
is a swift physical reminder
that though death's the price of otherness,

life's pleasure is much sharper
and its teeming forms increase
only because earth has two sexes.
An old man talks to a cock pheasant,
brings daily bread.
'He's all alone,' he says.

The copper beech glows on the hill.
A boy goes up the burnt grass path
carrying a scarlet kite.
Draggled dogs paddle in the cattle pool.
Londoners call them
and their children home.
A giant poplar rustles
as the evening sunlight falls.

DEFEAT

1

On their separate, steaming dunghills
one populist crows at another
and arrogant cockerels everywhere
echo their ultra cock-a-doodle-doo,
boasting their daybreak of betrayal:
their battle won against the feared idea
of fairness for fellow creatures everywhere
with all that that entails.

I went out and wept bitterly.

The defeat is baffling. In an unsafe world
now this belief, this dream,
which through the ages has refused to die
and many gave their lives to realise,
becomes more than merely kind and sane;
if it fails, for dear humanity
darkness falls.

Yet to affirm it now is sneered at
as naive, dismissed as naff, uncool.
Those braying victors' taunts will echo
round the cold, deserted earth
indefinitely, and no one remain to grieve,
when our species is long dead
with all that it achieved abandoned.

2

Meanwhile morning has risen,
the bright and the beautiful morning again.
As it softly wipes my eyes, I see
blue sky and my plane trees turning gold,
hear milk bottles clank, greetings,
doors slam as people leave for work.
London's awake. The least the pure fool
can do is keep speaking.
The least a poet can do is warn.

THE PURPLE-HEADED MOUNTAIN

I am flotsam of the great defeat
on the ugly flooding that has covered us.
Day after day, now tearlessly
I cry inside for the ground we lost,
the hope they've tried to make undreamable,
while fashionable clerks betray.
England, my desolate home, I feel for you.
And far away, I mourn the battering
of that brave small country once a beacon.
I lament for our whole plundered planet
and our poor people crucified.
Are we redeemable?

Wounded I went West,
back into the womb of my mother
the Great Rowbarrow and rested
in her, back to earth.
I could die here in this country of my desire.

From near a spring I drink
the crystal liquid that refreshes me.
I follow it flowing over red brown stones
through the combe it formed,
where few people come.
As the water forces its way
down different drops and gaps,
it makes music with different notes
tinkle, burble, gurgle, rush,
with counterpoint from birds' distinctive calls.
Between rocks with mossy tops
I see three clear jets meet and plait.

Young bracken uncurling smells of Eden.
Whorts are fruiting, heather coming out,
its colour answered both by foxgloves,
that even sprout on a little stony beach,
and thistles among reeds along the banks.
On the comfortable soft turf
the golden echo to the purple
is rock rose and birdsfoot trefoil.

After two streams and their combes combine,
on a wider knoll in the scant shade
of rowan and scraggy hawthorn.
stand seven wild ponies,
summer-glossy all the same dun brown,
six mares and a stallion grazing.
I feel the magic here enthral me,
that it might hold me here forever.
The thought of roaring London now defeats me.

As I walk another time along the top,
again meeting scarcely anyone,
a flock of adolescents suddenly appear,
from which one boy bounds towards me
in sleek shorts and trainers.
He is fleet, moon-faced and handsome,
the first black skin I have seen on Dunkery.

'All right?' he greets me.
'All right.' I reply.
'Where you from?'
'London,' I say.
'Cool. Me too. What part?'
'Camden Town.'
'Cool. I come from Dulwich.'

He continues up towards the Beacon,
turns and adds:
'I know a song about Camden Town Station.'
And runs on his way singing.

Why should I bless him unawares?
Were waters breaking, draining?
Was he Rainbow? Mercury?
Messenger from the Goddess?
Angel of Resurrection?

(In my head I heard a voice:
For you this demi-paradise is time out,
though others live here, work for peanuts.
Your place is elsewhere yet a while.)

Clearly at least, a summons back to town,
that strangely seems to have renewed
my strength to struggle on.

GOING TO WORK

Rushing to teach in Tower Hamlets
on the Docklands Light Railway from Bank
out of darkness by the lengthy steep haul
to the high viaduct's mean December daylight,
reaching Shadwell,
I nod to the friendly poplar flaring
up and over the freezing platform
on the Cable Street side,
its patient enormous life a reminder
of all it has seen.

In the dinky compartment
sharp-suited solid or wide boys,
distinct from messier mortals and locals,
read the *Telegraph, Times* and *Mail.*
This morning's front pages flame scarlet
after misty *brumaire*,
as marchers are massing impatient
in Paris against privatisation.

Pianissimo under my breath
I whistle 'The People's Flag'.
Some glance up askance
but none of them catches me at it,
retreat to their papers with growing unease,
as the whistling persists past Limehouse Basin.
Now Canary Wharf rears
its arrogant concrete angles
and the alphaville track's undulating
into divergent skyways.

'Passengers for the Island
stay on this train.
Change here for Beckton and Poplar,'
says the cockney loudspeaker.
As I alight with my teacher satchel
I add the announcement:
'Red Flags are flying in Paris,'
and am gratified by suppressed gasps.

ENGLISH LESSON

In an old LCC classroom in Stepney
with cream-washed walls and pipework,
dingy windows with frosted panes,
from a proud tradition of East End printers,
artisans, cream of a difficult craft,
students today seeking skills in computing —
graphics and typesetting —
wrestle with an English assignment
on an grey cold winter afternoon:
Describe how you feel about
somewhere in London — happy or grim
can be prose or poem.

A volunteer to read?
The first to come up leaps over his table
like a steeplechaser — a tricky feat
imitated with daft enthusiasm
by each one after. Some
express better than others the pain
and pleasure of their city
but how I enjoy the panache
with which they go for it,
picking up colt legs to clear the hurdle,
shy of exposure, but showing their bottle.
I wish I could bet on the life they get.

LIKE

On occasions it is a shock
when my daughter or my son
strikes me as exactly like me
but is not me.
On other days they may behave
in ways so alien to me
that the fact is a mystery.
They grow up and go off by themselves,
taking something of me with them
as well as their achieved defining otherness.

And curiously, having grown-up children
whom I might meet as strangers in the street,
I find I look on other Londoners
and listen to each distinctive tone of voice,
with fresh senses, a new feeling
of familiarity in strangeness,
closeness in separation,
likeness in difference, like poetry.
Life feels warmer but often rougher,
more uncomfortable.

My children could not mature
without cutting loose and getting away.
Neither can anyone who clings to God
as father. Let him go. Let him dwindle.
It seems I see humanity in sharper focus
as a mother of tall fellow citizens;
I appreciate and dread that as they spread
one day I must decrease and what matters,
like it or not, is more than family
or the individual.

THE DIVINE IMAGE

In 1975 E.P. Thompson
met the last Muggletonian,
who gave him access to their archive.
Thompson concluded that Blake's mother,
Catherine Hermitage,
was probably one of them.

The Muggletonians believed
that when Mary conceived Jesus
God became a mortal man
and on the cross he died.
Insight it was God that is finished.
Humanity rises again.

The mystery of Christmas:
God we set in heaven
beyond our scope
has come down
and it is down to us.

The mystery of the cross:
God we created alien
above the human
has suffered death like us,
returned to earth like seed.

The Easter mystery:
word of utmost hope
born of woman, killed, denied,
has risen indeed
and it is up to us.

PRIVATE HELL

Hell is that furious roaring:
Ignored, ignored, ignored.
Hell is that suffocating soundlessness:
I am utterly alone.

Hell is that thick glaucous glass window
through which I see others distorted,
grinning unpleasantly,
cavorting in the garden.

One way vision: they do not see me.
Insulation: they do not hear me.
Or maybe dismiss me as familiar blur,
goldfish mouthing what they want to hear.

Hell is the bleak musty basement
where I disintegrate
into a heap of disconnected bits
leaking and rusting in dim grime.

The boiler is there
that supplies power to my house,
requiring regular service.

If I ignore it, it might explode.
Sometimes I have to go down
but I live upstairs.

BODY OF WORK

Where is the stone with my name on it?
What is the word that is me?
Have I been faithful? I don't know.
Who is that child of five
in cotton frock and little white socks,
sat holding the reins on a huge horse,
Fitz Fritz, my father's favourite?
He detested Nazi Germany
but was the kind of Englishman
who would not dream of altering
his best-loved animal's German-sounding name
throughout the war. 'That's what he's called.'
(German prisoners worked on our farm,
I sat with them by their camp fire
and they made wooden toys for my brother and me.)
I look at the photo. It is me but am I she?

Who is that girl in her twenties
in miniscule skirt and frivolous hat,
light-heartedly, seriously reading the gospel
at a way-out wedding in Kentish Town,
(celebrated in the Aquinas Hall
by a tubby Dominican friar
who played 'Ring-a-Roses' at Porton Down)?
Actually she is quite beautiful
but I don't recall feeling that.
Now I am over fifty. Damn, I missed it!
I have the same name but how am I she?

It was about then I had begun
to write verse. Re-read today,
it's the voice of a young woman
now gone, but I hear myself speak.
My first published poem's first line
was: *Yes, worship the word.*
(It was also translated into German
so what word was that?)
Sometimes all I have written
seems like a heap of straw I can't spin,
or brown leaves blowing.

But it can be printed in a book
and that is a body of work in which,
unlike my photoed body, the years co-exist.
I haven't yet seen its final shape.
How odd. I never imagined my struggle
to articulate a coherence
answerable to my fellow mortals,
not an eternal ear,
would take that peculiar form.

Though it may be art, poetry isn't pure,
because the most important thing
is not how prettily it's written.
It is a distillation, but of what fruit?
What human quality rooted in what earth?
Bitter juniper has mothered a suicidal gin.
It matters what I mean
and where I stand, and that my words
are what I witness with.

Still, a poem isn't a poem
if it just airs my views.
It must utter who I am,
and as you do me the kindness
of appreciating the details of my world
(and as I do the same for you),
we act on the belief
that the delicious intractable particularity —
not that we like it all or equally —
is what makes life on our suffering planet
worthwhile. What is lovable
is what makes it poetry.
When death has closed my book,
will the body of work be complete?
If my name on the stone
is the title, what does it say?

GOTHIC

'I cannot kill but I can cancel you,'
the cruel stepmother gloats and gets the girl,
who must contain her rage in a locked cell,
condemned as dangerous criminal who might do
such damage that her father too would hate
her, then all the world repudiate
her, so give her vindicated torturer
the go ahead to get rid of her;
without a chance to answer, hustle all
that daughter down to the dark place
where no one ever hears her cries —
increasingly they're inarticulate
because she suffers the unspeakable.

The plot succeeded but not totally.
The daughter foiled it by becoming split
in two, but chained together at the heart
by savage razor wire invisibly.
From roarer banned behind the heavy oak
the tie fed through the keyhole, stretched to hook
fast, however far the other strove
to be herself and live her life and love.
Day after day she did, but if an unlucky
conjunction jabbed this wound, it bled,
tightened the wire, tugged roarer out of bed.
I must get out — all the old ache awoke:
Sunlight, save me, soothe me, set me free.

But this creature's ugly and repels all friends,
unreachable, a yowling giant child,
destructive of civil gatherings, rude and wild,
only able to consider its own ends.
Even its twin's ashamed and says: 'Lie down!'
Sometimes she speaks in her own parents' tone.
Still, if she breaks the linkage both will die;
she knows this well and knows well why.
The roarer is half herself, her energy; her mild
keen weeks of work would not survive
severed from the feral forces of her life.
Can they ever burst free from their prison,
rejoin the whole and welcome home and hold?

BECAUSE

God is no more.
Then is humanity
fit to adore?
Apparently not.
So why believe in it?

I believe because I love,
believe in what I love.
Love sees value,
gives value,
sees it as due.
Seeing as acknowledgment,
giving: solidarity.

I believe in human life
on earth our home
in a single breath
because I value it.
Faith
whose reason
is material.

I loathe the waste
and abhor the horror
our species
have done and do,
the mass murderous market,
the miserable profit motive,
most of all because

I know the pleasure
of being alive
we can imagine for everyone
in a harmonious order,
the comfort that
fellow feeling fumbles for
as fundamental.

I do not mean
I believe humanity
will achieve it.
I do mean
I believe we can.

Poetry reminds the tongue
of that familiar
taste of utopia,
homecoming feast
wafting to make the mouth water,

when its word and witness
console the hungry
and hopeless as I have been,
by its earthly promise,
prefiguring a future.

A sherbet fountain clue
to a lost afternoon,
heavenly blue
with you my love
in the birch wood.

Long ago.
Over.
A dreamlike memory.
But not nothing.
Love is the meaning.

THE EXCLUDED

Standing on London Bridge on a dreary day
I looked down at the grey river.
I entered the crying.
I heard the keen agony of the lonely,
the roaring of the ignored,
the fury of the defeated,
the tortured screaming an ultimate No,
protests at all the unjust lessening,
weakening as the life force ebbed away.
Wasted. In that chorus, one note
in my own voice told me how it was.

Thousand upon thousand
of the excluded crowded in,
rank on rank of sorrow.
I had not thought there would be so many
uttering that intolerable sound,
beyond the range of the authorities,
who did not have ears to hear it.
But that ultrasonic pitch had greater power
than any laser to shatter the city,
with all its gates and bridges,
however magnificent and strong.

See how it stands desolate
like a hut in a cucumber field,
possession of the hedgehog and pools of tears.
Will that tomorrow ever come
when the crying is comforted,
the weeping wiped away?

Will the dispossessed inherit the earth,
the beautiful pillars of peace be built?
Will eager boys climb trees to watch
and hang like fruit on a clear blue night,
while multitudes stand on London Bridge
exulting in the Easter fireworks,
starbursts flowering for the festival?

TO MY OLD FRIEND HUGO MEYNELL ON RECEIVING A PRESENT OF HIS BOOK *IS CHRISTIANITY TRUE?*

Hugo, I've read your book,
Is Christianity True?
You still answer that it is,
not just 'profoundly true', you say —
how like you — but literally so.
Now I can hardly recall the me
you knew in Leeds in the early sixties, who
having studied Greek and Hebrew with a will,
wholeheartedly agreed with you
and had preached it in Hyde Park
as a know-all teenager,
like you, appalling my family
when I turned RC.

I left the Church
a quarter of a century ago
because I no longer could support
a literal God or resurrection,
and anyway was on the pill
and did not want priests' fingers
in my soul.
Like you, I am literal-minded,
thought church membership
committed me to certain assertions:
if Christ is not risen our faith is vain.
But now I no longer believed,
now took a different view, so I left.
Your book reminds me of my callow youth.

Yet in another way I am,
I feel the same,
one and the same Dinah,
only older, calmer,
fiercer and more radical,
driven, I believe, to conclusions,
to my roots in earth,
by one and the same
logic of *logos ensarkikos*
incarnate word (or in the feminine, wisdom).

Hugo, I don't write this as apologetic.
Besides, I believe you unbudgeable
and you know I admire you
as one who has endured those years in exile
and spoken out when you knew you should.
I write as a conversation.
You know what I am talking about
because we are the same kind of animal —
or similar (that little 'i' Gibbon mocked).
Like my pony Ringlets, who would sense
and avoid an Exmoor bog,
we distrust that lurid green,
postmodernist slough of despond.

I would translate 'mites fac et castos'
not as: 'meek and chaste' —
I don't want to be either —
but: 'make us humble, single-minded.'
Though I fall short I still seek
above all for that.
You see what I mean.
I write because
you will listen and understand.

Blake, asked where his visions came from,
tapped his forehead and said: 'Here!'
I agree all gods reside in the human breast
and are created by the poetic genius,
which is also the spirit of prophecy.
Poetry is incarnate word
by which all gods are made.

Poets make them,
discerning earthly powers which their
'enlarged and numerous senses' have perceived.
(For everyone whose soul is not a clod
has visions . . .) Mystics and prophets
may be the truest poets.
What mystics see: *love is the meaning*
has consequences, urging prophets
to speak out, denounce, announce.
The christian story is a subversive poem.

In it I believe the incarnation
means that the God we set in heaven above
has come back down, become a man;
the divine is a human face,
a body that suffers
and is warm and soft.

The crucifixion means that God has died,
the word is poured out.
In the resurrection word rises again
and its glory that we gave to God
is now redeemed as wholly human,
yours and mine, not alien.
Ascending, human wisdom
reclaims its own high imagining,

the heart's hope of utopia
unseats the Nobodaddy aloft.

Christ is still crucified on earth today
while the poor are killed by the sin of the world —
greed for profit at any loss.
The struggle continues;
now his resurrection recurs
when the crucified people rise
to overcome those who discount them.
This is the conquest of death and hell
that will sing the ultimate alleluia:
O mors, ero mors tua,
morsus tuus ero, inferne!

The parousia, New Jerusalem,
the change beyond the change
(it doesn't have to be described
in christian terms),
depends on human action,
so it may or may not happen.

It means the hope fulfilled,
faith as something understood,
not up there, but down here,
heaven *now here* where we are at home
and can be happy
if an economy of grace,
humanity's shape shining
(beauty so old and so new),
word of justice,
become deed on earth.

And as we are in time, not eternity,
as we are mortal,
even if we make the dream come true,
it will be fragile,
liable to damage, souring and spoiling.
There will always be work to do.
Unlike a static heaven above
boredom won't be a problem.

That is its outcome:
the logic of the incarnate word
drives me to atheism,
drives me to humanism,
drives me to socialism.
It seeks what it lacks
to complete the poem.
It does not supply
the political detail
or resolve the dialectic
to work it out.

For love of this word, this wisdom
that I have seen,
recognised, delighted in
and followed as I could
(as you have Hugo,
brave and lonely lately):

I value human life,
I value life on earth,
I value the earth.
Therefore I value kindness,
I value fairness and its sweet-sharp fruit
(which we also taste in poetry),
that achieved tranquillity of order:
peace.

Human life is of infinite
worth, for what it is
and for what it may become —
the necessary goodness that we stored
in a God we made,
like delicious food
in a deep freeze,
waiting to be embodied in us,
to fill up what is wanting.

And the greatest of these is love,
of the physical body,
of the social body in harmony.
Otherwise before long: barbarism,
with the millennium:
no supper ever again.

RISK

The granite steps carved in the cave
descend to the deep salt pool.
Dive in and swim under the arch of rock:
you drown or reach open sea.
The beach warms the soles of your feet.
Sweet voices perfume the air.
Red roses are rooted in rage,
love's dangerous, rich energy.

PRESSURE OF LIFE

Arrangements, conflicts, contracts, creditors
crowd my busy head to bursting.
I thread through packed thrusting punters,
a limp resident out for a bit of fruit
from Inverness Street Market,
who failed to remember it is Saturday
when Camden Lock is chock-a-block.
Back home I eat apples of exhaustion.

Later as I listen to leaves brushing
the azure-golden autumn weather
and watch a couple of soft white swans
glide slowly past on a Kenwood pond,
I let myself be the rippling waters,
become the motion and the spirit that impels,
the same breath that earlier agitated to ugliness
the throng of jostling bargain-hunters
and me among them.

IN AVERY HILL PARK

A huge oak in the hedge
burns October gold-ochre
on the edge of the playing field,
whose mown grasses
recent mild rain has urged
up to about three inches,
before they slow for winter.

A fresh breeze pushes them sideways,
sun on each green blade,
glittering.

Sat here in my fifty-fourth year
at my lunchtime ease,
I feast each sense. I listen
to sparrows and little rustles,
sniff bonfire and loam on the autumn
pure blue air that holds me
with these my planetary companions.

Belonging with them to earth,
I feel it intensely alive,
turning.

THIS

The plane tree is a naked giant now,
its lacy and bobbled
delicate tracery revealed,
sharp against blue. Shape.
Its huge soul winters out.
I absorb its quiet in admiration.

How bodied the pigeon is
when it perches on bare branch.
Yesterday I saw one sat,
as if rehearsing
the twelve days of Christmas,
but in a plum tree.

Its beady amber eye gleamed
on the deep gold fruits,
little magic lanterns still attached,
though all the leaves had gone.
The birdness of that bird:
its being made me glad.

Bird and tree are
and so are we.
Who needs God
when we share such selfhood?

Isn't God merely a codeword
meaning our human kind of self
not only is
but may become
what we imagine
in love and poetry?

MAYTIME

He and she walked out into a May meadow
and made love under a flowering tree.
The sun lit the buttercups
among the new green grass
and shone on the shape of each fresh leaf
pushed out by a rush of juice.
A bird chorus described the sweetness
up to the soft surrounding blue.
The ground was damp and smelt of home.

My beloved is agile and strong
and delicate as a leaping deer.
Come to me. Come.
Then in bliss they rested.

She cupped in her hand
what was now as little and sticky
as a just hatched chick.
Uccellino, he told her and smiled
irresistibly. She kissed him.
After a while: *Eppur si muove* –
it *does* move – he said.

Happy, they laughed
and – honouring great Galileo
who fought for the truth
about what our earth is and does,
against false religion,
and cocked a snook
at the priests in black gowns
on his deathbed –
they made love again.

NOTES

Page

9: 'Trees Be Company' is the title of a dialect poem by William Barnes, in *Selected Poems* (Penguin Classics, 1994).

21: The pheasant's call echoes Blake's 'Song of Liberty' (12) at the end of *The Marriage of Heaven and Hell:* 'Look up! Look up! O citizen of London, enlarge thy countenance.'

31: 'Defeat' was written after far-right populist Arnoldo Alemán won the Nicaraguan elections in November 1996. Of course, he is not the only one to whom the poem refers. A peculiarly repellent local manifestation was Michael Portillo's birthday party in the Ally Pally.

33: It is said locally that Mrs C.F. Alexander wrote the hymn 'All Things Bright and Beautiful' from Grabbist Hill, Dunster, and that the distant 'purple-headed mountain' was Dunkery, the highest point on Exmoor.

40: E. P. Thompson, who once defined himself as a Muggletonian Marxist, describes his meeting with the last Muggletonian in his *Witness against the Beast* (Cambridge 1993).

52: Hugo Meynell, *Is Christianity True?* (Geoffrey Chapman, London 1994).

53: The Nicene Creed, elaborated in fourth and fifth century Church Councils, declared that Jesus was 'of the same substance' *(homoousios)* as the Father. The doctrine was fiercely debated by Arians and others, some of whom produced the formula 'of like substance' *(homoiousios)*. This provoked Gibbon's famous sneer that the whole of Europe was in turmoil over an 'i'.

53: 'Mites fac et castos' is a line from the hymn to Mary, *Ave Maris Stella* .

55: *O mors* . . . (Oh death, I will be your death, Hell, I will be your deadly sting.) *First Antiphon* for the office of Lauds on Easter Saturday.

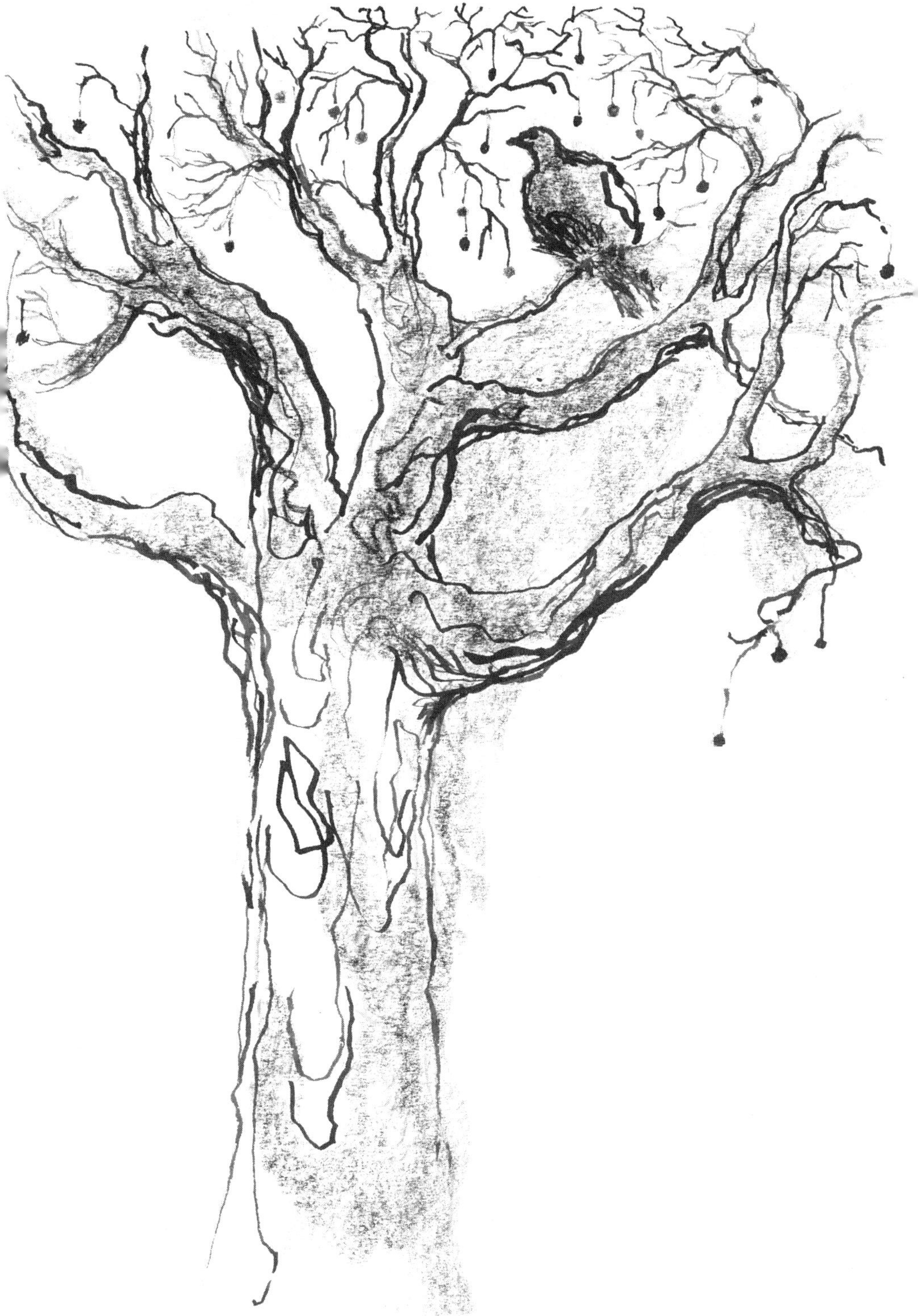